MASTERING
ON A LOOM

MW00883711

A Comprehensive Guide for Beginners to
Advanced Crafters

Chris Duncan

Table of Content

CHAPTER ONE

Introduction

Welcome to the world of bead weaving on the loom! Whether you're a seasoned crafter looking to expand your skills or a curious beginner eager to dive into a new creative endeavor, this book is your comprehensive guide to mastering the art of bead weaving on a loom.

Bead weaving is a timeless craft with a rich history that spans cultures and continents.

From ancient civilizations to contemporary artisans, beads have been cherished for their beauty, symbolism, and versatility. Today, bead weaving continues to captivate and inspire crafters around the world with its endless possibilities for creativity and self-expression.

In this book, we'll embark on a journey together, exploring everything you need to know to become proficient in bead weaving on the loom. We'll start with the basics, from selecting the right loom and beads to setting up your workspace and mastering fundamental techniques. As we progress, we'll delve into more advanced stitches, patterns, and design concepts, empowering you to create intricate and stunning beadwork with confidence.

Whether you're interested in crafting intricate jewelry pieces, embellishing accessories, or adorning your home with unique decor items, bead weaving on the loom offers endless possibilities for artistic expression.

Gather your tools, unleash your creativity, and let's embark on this exciting bead weaving adventure together.

History

The art of bead weaving on a loom has a rich and diverse history that spans cultures and civilizations across the globe. While the exact origins of bead weaving are difficult to pinpoint, archaeological evidence suggests that humans have been crafting with beads for thousands of years.

One of the earliest examples of beadwork dates back to ancient Egypt, where intricate bead designs adorned jewelry, clothing, and ceremonial objects. These early artisans used a variety of materials, including glass, faience, and semi-precious stones, to create stunning beadwork that reflected their status and beliefs.

Bead weaving also has a long tradition in Native American cultures, where it played a significant role in both personal adornment and ceremonial practices. Native American beadwork is renowned for its intricate designs, vibrant colors, and symbolic significance, with each bead and pattern carrying deep cultural meaning.

In Europe, bead weaving flourished during the Middle Ages and Renaissance periods, particularly among the nobility and clergy. Elaborate beadwork adorned garments, accessories, and religious artifacts, showcasing the wealth and status of the wearer.

During the Victorian era, bead weaving experienced a resurgence in popularity, with intricate beaded jewelry and accessories becoming fashionable among the upper classes. This period saw the rise of beadwork techniques such as tambour beading and bead embroidery, which added texture and dimension to designs.

In the 20th century, bead weaving underwent a revival as artisans rediscovered and reinterpreted traditional techniques while also experimenting with new materials and styles. The rise of bead societies, workshops, and publications fueled interest in the craft, leading to a resurgence of creativity and innovation.

Today, bead weaving on the loom continues to thrive as a beloved craft practiced by artisans and hobbyists around the world. With the advent of modern tools, materials, and techniques, contemporary bead weavers are pushing the boundaries of traditional beadwork, creating innovative designs that blend old-world charm with contemporary flair.

As we delve into the world of bead weaving in this book, we pay homage to the rich history and cultural heritage of this ancient craft while also celebrating its enduring appeal and evolution in the modern age. From ancient Egypt to the present day, bead weaving on the loom remains a timeless art form that continues to inspire and delight crafters of all ages and backgrounds.

Benefits and Advantage

Bead weaving on a loom offers a wide range of benefits and advantages for crafters of all skill levels.

Precision and Consistency: Using a loom allows for precise placement of beads, resulting in uniformity and consistency in your designs. This is especially beneficial for creating intricate patterns and geometric shapes with ease.

Efficiency and Speed: Bead weaving on a loom can be more efficient and faster than other beadwork techniques, particularly when working on larger projects or repeating patterns. The loom holds the warp threads taut, allowing you to focus solely on weaving the beads.

Versatility: Loom bead weaving offers endless possibilities for creativity and experimentation. From jewelry and accessories to home decor and embellishments, the versatility of bead weaving on a loom allows you to explore a wide range of projects and applications.

Accessibility: Bead weaving on a loom is accessible to crafters of all skill levels, from beginners to experienced artisans. With basic techniques and a few essential tools, anyone can learn to create beautiful beadwork on a loom, making it an inclusive and welcoming craft.

Relaxation and Mindfulness: Engaging in bead weaving on a loom can be a therapeutic and meditative experience. The repetitive motion of threading beads onto the warp threads can help calm the mind, reduce stress, and promote mindfulness.

Customization and Personalization: One of the greatest advantages of bead weaving on a loom is the ability to customize and personalize your creations. Whether you're designing jewelry for yourself or creating gifts for loved ones, bead weaving allows you to tailor your designs to suit your individual style and preferences.

Sense of Achievement: Completing a bead weaving project on a loom can be incredibly satisfying and rewarding. Seeing your vision come to life as you weave each bead into place provides a sense of accomplishment and pride in your craftsmanship.

Overall, bead weaving on a loom offers a unique combination of precision, efficiency, versatility, and creativity that makes it a truly fulfilling and enjoyable craft. Whether you're a seasoned bead weaver or just starting out, exploring the world of loom bead weaving is sure to inspire and delight your creative spirit.

CHAPTER TWO

Essential Materials and Tools

Before diving into bead weaving on a loom, it's essential to gather the right materials and tools to ensure a smooth and enjoyable crafting experience.

Loom: Choose a loom suitable for bead weaving, such as a bead loom, Mirrix loom, or a simple homemade loom. Looms come in various sizes and styles, so select one that suits your project needs and preferences.

Beads: Choose beads suitable for loom weaving, such as seed beads, Delica beads, or cylinder beads. Beads come in different sizes, shapes, colors, and finishes, allowing you to customize your designs to your liking.

Thread or Beading Cord: Use strong and durable thread or beading cord specifically designed for bead weaving. Nylon thread, Fireline, or Nymo are popular choices for securing beads on the loom.

Needles: Choose beading needles with a fine, flexible, and thin shaft to easily pass through the small bead holes. Select needles that fit the size of your beads and thread, ensuring smooth weaving without snagging.

Scissors: Keep a pair of sharp scissors handy for cutting thread, cord, and any excess material during your bead weaving projects.

Beading Mat or Tray: Use a soft beading mat or tray to prevent beads from rolling away and to keep your workspace organized. A beading mat also provides a cushioned surface for comfortable weaving.

Beading Thread Conditioner: Optionally, use a thread conditioner such as beeswax or Thread Heaven to strengthen and lubricate your thread, making it more resistant to fraying and tangling.

Measuring Tape or Ruler: Have a measuring tape or ruler on hand to ensure accurate sizing and spacing of your bead weaving projects, especially when working on specific patterns or designs.

Bead Containers: Use small containers or organizers to store and separate your beads by color, size, or type, keeping them easily accessible and neatly organized during your bead weaving sessions.

Design Graph or Pattern: Have a design graph or pattern handy to guide your bead placement and color choices, especially for complex designs or repeating patterns.

By gathering these essential materials and tools, you'll be well-equipped to embark on your bead weaving journey with confidence and creativity. Whether you're weaving intricate jewelry pieces, embellishing accessories, or adorning home decor items, having the right supplies at your fingertips will ensure a successful and enjoyable bead weaving experience.

Types of Looms and Their Features
Bead Loom:

Traditional bead looms consist of a rectangular frame with two or more rollers or dowels at each end to hold the warp threads.

Features adjustable tension screws or knobs to regulate the tightness of the warp threads.

Typically used for weaving flat beadwork, such as bracelets, belts, and tapestries.

Easy to use for beginners and offers versatility for creating both simple and intricate designs.

Mirrix Loom:

Mirrix looms are modern, high-quality bead looms designed for precision and versatility.

Features a metal or wooden frame with tensioning devices, such as springs or clips, to maintain consistent tension on the warp threads.

Offers shedding devices, such as shedding bars or treadles, for weaving more complex patterns and designs.

Allows for weaving both flat and dimensional beadwork, including tapestries, bags, and sculptural pieces.

Comes in various sizes and configurations to suit different project needs and preferences.

Homemade Loom:

Homemade looms can be crafted from everyday materials such as cardboard, wood, or PVC pipe.

Features a simple frame or structure to hold the warp threads in place.

Provides an affordable option for beginners or crafters looking to experiment with bead weaving before investing in a commercial loom.

Allows for customization in size and design to accommodate different project requirements.

Beading Loom Kits:

Beading loom kits are beginner-friendly sets that include a small loom, beads, thread, needles, and instructions.

Designed for simplicity and ease of use, making them ideal for beginners or younger crafters.

Features pre-designed patterns or templates to guide users through their first bead weaving projects.

Offers a convenient and affordable way to get started with bead weaving without needing to purchase individual supplies.

Features to Consider:

Size: Choose a loom size that suits the scale of your projects, from small-scale jewelry pieces to larger tapestries or wall hangings.

Tensioning Mechanism: Look for a loom with adjustable tensioning mechanisms to ensure even tension on the warp threads throughout your weaving.

Shedding Devices: Consider looms with shedding devices for weaving more complex patterns and designs, such as Mirrix looms with shedding bars or treadles.

Portability: If you plan to travel with your loom or weave on the go, consider the portability and weight of the loom for easy transport.

Durability: Opt for a sturdy and well-constructed loom that can withstand regular use and provide long-lasting reliability.

Price: Compare the features and prices of different looms to find one that fits your budget while meeting your needs and preferences.

Experiment with different looms to discover which one best suits your style, projects, and crafting goals.

Setting Up The Workspace

Setting up your workspace for bead weaving on a loom is essential for a comfortable and efficient crafting experience.

Choose a Well-Lit Area: Select a well-lit area with ample natural or artificial light to reduce eye strain and enhance visibility while working on your bead weaving projects.

Flat Surface: Use a sturdy and flat surface, such as a table or desk, to set up your loom and work comfortably. Ensure the surface is clean and free of clutter to prevent beads from rolling away or getting lost.

Bead Mat or Tray: Place a soft beading mat or tray on your workspace to prevent beads from rolling and to keep them organized. The mat also provides a cushioned surface for comfortable weaving and protects your work surface from scratches.

Organize Your Supplies: Keep your beads, thread, needles, and other supplies within easy reach and neatly organized on your workspace. Use small containers, organizers, or compartments to separate and store your beads by color, size, or type for quick access during your projects.

Tools and Accessories: Arrange your tools and accessories, such as scissors, measuring tape, needles, and thread conditioner, within reach on your workspace. Having your tools readily available will streamline your workflow and minimize interruptions during your bead weaving sessions.

Comfortable Seating: Choose a comfortable chair or stool that provides adequate support and allows you to sit at the appropriate height relative to your loom. Maintain good posture while weaving to prevent discomfort or strain on your back, neck, and shoulders.

Adjustable Lighting: If working with artificial lighting, consider using an adjustable desk lamp with a flexible arm and adjustable brightness settings to customize the lighting conditions to your preferences and project requirements.

Workspace Organization: Keep your workspace organized and clutter-free by tidying up after each bead weaving session.

Dispose of any waste materials, secure loose threads, and return unused beads and supplies to their storage containers to maintain a clean and organized workspace.

Warping the Loom

Warping the loom is the crucial first step in bead weaving, as it sets the foundation for your project.

Prepare Your Loom: Set up your loom on a flat, stable surface, ensuring that it's securely anchored and won't move during the warping process. Adjust the tensioning mechanisms if needed to create a taut and even warp.

Determine Warp Length: Decide on the desired length of your warp threads, taking into account the dimensions of your project and any additional length needed for finishing and securing the ends. Cut a piece of beading thread or cord to the desired length, adding a few extra inches for tying off and securing the ends.

Attach the Warp Thread: Tie one end of the warp thread to the anchor point on the loom, such as a roller or dowel, using a secure knot, such as a double knot or slip knot. Leave a tail of a few inches to weave in later.

Thread the Warp: Pass the warp thread through the designated spacing on the loom, following the predetermined pattern or spacing guide. Use a needle or shuttle to guide the warp thread through the slots or holes in the loom, alternating between over and under the raised warp threads.

Maintain Tension: As you thread the warp, maintain even tension on the threads to ensure they're straight and taut. Adjust the tensioning mechanisms on the loom as needed to keep the warp threads evenly spaced and under tension.

Secure the End: Once you've threaded the desired number of warp threads, tie off the end of the warp thread to the anchor point on the opposite end of the loom using a secure knot. Trim any excess thread, leaving a tail to weave in later.

Check Tension and Alignment: Before proceeding to bead weaving, double-check the tension and alignment of the warp threads to ensure they're uniform and evenly spaced across the loom. Make any necessary adjustments to the tensioning mechanisms or warp threads as needed.

Begin Bead Weaving: With the loom warped and ready to go, you're now ready to start bead weaving! Follow your chosen pattern or design, weaving beads onto the warp threads according to your desired pattern or design.

CHAPTER THREE

Basic Techniques

Plain Weave:

Set Up Your Loom: Begin by setting up your loom according to the manufacturer's instructions. Ensure that the warp threads are evenly spaced and under tension.

Thread Your Needle: Thread a beading needle with your desired thread or beading cord. Knot the end of the thread to prevent beads from slipping off.

Start Weaving: Bring your needle up through the first warp thread from the bottom to the top of the loom. Slide a bead down the thread until it rests against the warp thread.

Pass the Needle: Insert the needle down through the next warp thread, moving over the bead you just added. Pull the thread snugly to secure the bead in place.

Repeat: Continue weaving in this manner, adding one bead per warp thread, until you reach the end of the row. Make sure to maintain even tension and spacing between the beads.

Finish the Row: When you reach the end of the row, pass the needle around the last warp thread and bring it back up through the beads to secure them in place.

Weave Back: To begin the next row, weave the needle back through the beads in the opposite direction, passing over the beads you previously added and under the empty warp threads.

Continue Weaving: Repeat steps 3-7 for each subsequent row, alternating the direction of the weave with each pass to create a flat and stable beadwork.

Finishing Off: Once you've completed your desired length of beadwork, finish off the ends by weaving the thread through the beads to secure them in place. Secure the thread with a knot and trim any extra length.

Ladder Stitch:

Set Up Your Loom: Prepare your loom as described above, ensuring that the warp threads are evenly spaced and under tension.

Thread Your Needle: Thread a beading needle with your chosen thread or cord, and knot the end to prevent beads from slipping off.

Start Weaving: Bring your needle up through the first warp thread from the bottom to the top of the loom. Slide a bead down the thread until it rests against the warp thread.

Create the Ladder: Pass the needle back down through the same warp thread, positioning the bead in place. Then, bring the needle up through the next warp thread, without adding a bead.

Continue Adding Beads: Repeat step 3, adding a bead to the same warp thread, then pass the needle down through the next warp thread, skipping a thread each time.

Maintain Consistency: Ensure that each bead is positioned snugly against the warp threads and that the spacing between beads remains consistent throughout the row.

Finish the Row: When you reach the end of the row, pass the needle around the last warp thread and bring it back up through the beads to secure them in place.

Weave Back: To begin the next row, weave the needle back through the beads in the opposite direction, passing over the beads you previously added and under the empty warp threads.

Continue Weaving: Repeat steps 3-8 for each subsequent row, alternating the direction of the weave with each pass to create a stable ladder-like pattern.

Finishing Off: Once you've completed your desired length of beadwork, finish off the ends by weaving the thread through the beads to secure them in place. Secure the thread with a knot and trim any extra length.

Zigzag Weave:

Prepare Your Loom: Set up your loom according to the manufacturer's instructions, ensuring that the warp threads are evenly spaced and under tension.

Thread Your Needle: Thread a beading needle with your chosen thread or cord, and knot the end to prevent beads from slipping off.

Start Weaving: Begin by bringing your needle up through the first warp thread from the bottom to the top of the loom. Slide a bead down the thread until it rests against the warp thread.

Create the Zigzag Pattern: Pass the needle down through the next warp thread, then bring it up through the third warp thread. Add another bead to the thread and pass the needle down through the fourth warp thread.

Continue Weaving: Repeat step 4, alternating the direction of the weave with each pass to create a zigzag pattern. Ensure that each bead is positioned snugly against the warp threads and that the spacing between beads remains consistent throughout the row.

Finish the Row: When you reach the end of the row, pass the needle around the last warp thread and bring it back up through the beads to secure them in place.

Weave Back: To begin the next row, weave the needle back through the beads in the opposite direction, passing over the beads you previously added and under the empty warp threads.

Continue Weaving: Repeat steps 3-7 for each subsequent row, alternating the direction of the weave with each pass to maintain the zigzag pattern.

Finishing Off: Once you've completed your desired length of beadwork, finish off the ends by weaving the thread through the beads to secure them in place. Secure the thread with a knot and trim any extra length.

Brick Stitch:

Prepare Your Loom: Set up your loom as described above, ensuring that the warp threads are evenly spaced and under tension.

Thread Your Needle: Thread a beading needle with your chosen thread or cord, and knot the end to prevent beads from slipping off.

Start Weaving: Begin by bringing your needle up through the first warp thread from the bottom to the top of the loom. Slide a bead down the thread until it rests against the warp thread.

Create the Base Row: Pass the needle down through the same warp thread, positioning the bead in place. Then, bring the needle up through the next warp thread, without adding a bead.

Add Beads to the Base Row: Repeat step 3, adding a bead to the same warp thread, then pass the needle down through the next warp thread, skipping a thread each time.

Build Upward: Continue adding beads to the base row, alternating the placement of the beads to create a staggered or brick-like pattern. Ensure that each bead is positioned snugly against the warp threads.

Finish the Row: When you reach the end of the row, pass the needle around the last warp thread and bring it back up through the beads to secure them in place.

Weave Back: To begin the next row, weave the needle back through the beads in the opposite direction, passing over the beads you previously added and under the empty warp threads.

Continue Weaving: Repeat steps 3-8 for each subsequent row, alternating the direction of the weave with each pass to maintain the brick stitch pattern.

Finishing Off: Once you've completed your desired length of beadwork, finish off the ends by weaving the thread through the beads to secure them in place. Secure the thread with a knot and trim any extra length.

Herringbone Stitch:

Set Up Your Loom: Begin by setting up your loom according to the manufacturer's instructions, ensuring that the warp threads are evenly spaced and under tension.

Thread Your Needle: Thread a beading needle with your chosen thread or cord, and knot the end to prevent beads from slipping off.

Start Weaving: Bring your needle up through the first warp thread from the bottom to the top of the loom. Slide two beads down the thread until they rest against the warp thread.

Create the First Stitch: Pass the needle down through the next warp thread, then bring it up through the following warp thread. Pull the thread snugly to create the first herringbone stitch.

Continue Stitching: Add two more beads to the thread and pass the needle down through the next warp thread. Then, bring it up through the following two warp threads to create the next stitch.

Repeat: Repeat step 5, adding two beads and creating stitches across the entire row. Ensure that each pair of beads is positioned snugly against the warp threads and that the spacing between stitches remains consistent.

Finish the Row: When you reach the end of the row, pass the needle around the last warp thread and bring it back up through the beads to secure them in place.

Weave Back: To begin the next row, weave the needle back through the beads in the opposite direction, passing over the beads you previously added and under the empty warp threads.

Continue Weaving: Repeat steps 3-8 for each subsequent row, alternating the direction of the weave with each pass to maintain the herringbone stitch pattern.

Finishing Off: Once you've completed your desired length of beadwork, finish off the ends by weaving the thread through the beads to secure them in place. Secure the thread with a knot and trim any extra length.

Peyote Stitch:

Set Up Your Loom: Prepare your loom as described above, ensuring that the warp threads are evenly spaced and under tension.

Thread Your Needle: Thread a beading needle with your chosen thread or cord, and knot the end to prevent beads from slipping off.

Start Weaving: Begin by bringing your needle up through the first warp thread from the bottom to the top of the loom. Slide one bead down the thread until it rests against the warp thread.

Create the Base Row: Pass the needle down through the same warp thread, positioning the bead in place. Then, bring the needle up through the next warp thread, without adding a bead.

Add Beads to the Base Row: Repeat step 3, adding a bead to the same warp thread, then pass the needle down through the next warp thread, skipping a thread each time.

Build Upward: Continue adding beads to the base row, alternating the placement of the beads to create a staggered or brick-like pattern. Ensure that each bead is positioned snugly against the warp threads.

Finish the Row: When you reach the end of the row, pass the needle around the last warp thread and bring it back up through the beads to secure them in place.

Weave Back: To begin the next row, weave the needle back through the beads in the opposite direction, passing over the beads you previously added and under the empty warp threads.

Continue Weaving: Repeat steps 3-8 for each subsequent row, alternating the direction of the weave with each pass to maintain the peyote stitch pattern.

Finishing Off: Once you've completed your desired length of beadwork, finish off the ends by weaving the thread through the beads to secure them in place. Secure the thread with a knot and trim any extra length.

Advanced Techniques

Netting Stitch:

Set Up Your Loom: Begin by setting up your loom according to the manufacturer's instructions, ensuring that the warp threads are evenly spaced and under tension.

Thread Your Needle: Thread a beading needle with your chosen thread or cord, and knot the end to prevent beads from slipping off.

Start Weaving: Bring your needle up through the first warp thread from the bottom to the top of the loom. Slide three beads down the thread until they rest against the warp thread.

Create the First Unit: Pass the needle down through the next warp thread, then bring it up through the following warp thread. Slide two beads down the thread.

Form the Netting: Pass the needle down through the same warp thread you came up through, creating a loop around the previous unit of beads. Pull the thread snugly to tighten the loop.

Continue Weaving: Repeat steps 4-5, adding units of beads across the entire row. Ensure that each unit is positioned snugly against the warp threads and that the spacing between units remains consistent.

Finish the Row: When you reach the end of the row, pass the needle around the last warp thread and bring it back up through the beads to secure them in place.

Weave Back: To begin the next row, weave the needle back through the beads in the opposite direction, passing over the beads you previously added and under the empty warp threads.

Continue Weaving: Repeat steps 3-8 for each subsequent row, alternating the direction of the weave with each pass to maintain the netting stitch pattern.

Finishing Off: Once you've completed your desired length of beadwork, finish off the ends by weaving the thread through the beads to secure them in place. Secure the thread with a knot and trim any extra length.

Spiral Stitch:

Set Up Your Loom: Prepare your loom as described above, ensuring that the warp threads are evenly spaced and under tension.

Thread Your Needle: Thread a beading needle with your chosen thread or cord, and knot the end to prevent beads from slipping off.

Start Weaving: Begin by bringing your needle up through the first warp thread from the bottom to the top of the loom. Slide one bead down the thread until it rests against the warp thread.

Create the Base Row: Pass the needle down through the same warp thread, positioning the bead in place. Then, bring the needle up through the next warp thread, without adding a bead.

Add Beads to the Base Row: Repeat step 3, adding a bead to the same warp thread, then pass the needle down through the next warp thread, skipping a thread each time.

Build Upward: Continue adding beads to the base row, alternating the placement of the beads to create a staggered or brick-like pattern. Ensure that each bead is positioned snugly against the warp threads.

Form the Spiral: As you continue weaving, gradually increase or decrease the number of beads in each row to create a spiral pattern. Experiment with different bead counts and placements to achieve the desired effect.

Finish the Row: When you reach the end of the row, pass the needle around the last warp thread and bring it back up through the beads to secure them in place.

Weave Back: To begin the next row, weave the needle back through the beads in the opposite direction, passing over the beads you previously added and under the empty warp threads.

Continue Weaving: Repeat steps 3-8 for each subsequent row, adjusting the bead count and placement as needed to maintain the spiral stitch pattern.

Finishing Off: Once you've completed your desired length of beadwork, finish off the ends by weaving the thread through the beads to secure them in place. Secure the thread with a knot and trim any extra length.

St. Petersburg Stitch:

Set Up Your Loom: Begin by setting up your loom according to the manufacturer's instructions, ensuring that the warp threads are evenly spaced and under tension.

Thread Your Needle: Thread a beading needle with your chosen thread or cord, and knot the end to prevent beads from slipping off.

Start Weaving: Bring your needle up through the first warp thread from the bottom to the top of the loom. Slide two beads down the thread until they rest against the warp thread.

Create the First Unit: Pass the needle down through the next warp thread, then bring it up through the following warp thread. Slide one bead down the thread.

Form the First Loop: Pass the needle down through the same warp thread you came up through, creating a loop around the previous unit of beads. Pull the thread snugly to tighten the loop.

Add a Bead: Slide one bead down the thread, then pass the needle up through the next warp thread. Pull the thread snugly to position the bead next to the previous unit.

Continue Weaving: Repeat steps 4-6, alternating between adding units of beads and single beads across the entire row. Ensure that each bead is positioned snugly against the warp threads and that the spacing between units remains consistent.

Finish the Row: When you reach the end of the row, pass the needle around the last warp thread and bring it back up through the beads to secure them in place.

Weave Back: To begin the next row, weave the needle back through the beads in the opposite direction, passing over the beads you previously added and under the empty warp threads.

Continue Weaving: Repeat steps 3-9 for each subsequent row, alternating the direction of the weave with each pass to maintain the St. Petersburg stitch pattern.

Finishing Off: Once you've completed your desired length of beadwork, finish off the ends by weaving the thread through the beads to secure them in place. Secure the thread with a knot and trim any extra length.

Right-Angle Weave:

Set Up Your Loom: Prepare your loom as described above, ensuring that the warp threads are evenly spaced and under tension.

Thread Your Needle: Thread a beading needle with your chosen thread or cord, and knot the end to prevent beads from slipping off.

Start Weaving: Begin by bringing your needle up through the first warp thread from the bottom to the top of the loom. Slide four beads down the thread until they rest against the warp thread.

Form the Base Unit: Pass the needle down through the same warp thread you came up through, creating a loop around the previous unit of beads. Pull the thread snugly to tighten the loop.

Add a Bead: Slide one bead down the thread, then pass the needle up through the next warp thread. Pull the thread snugly to position the bead next to the previous unit.

Create the Next Unit: Pass the needle down through the same warp thread you came up through, creating a loop around the previous unit of beads. Pull the thread snugly to tighten the loop.

Continue Weaving: Repeat steps 5-6, alternating between adding single beads and creating units of beads across the entire row. Ensure that each bead is positioned snugly against the warp threads and that the spacing between units remains consistent.

Finish the Row: When you reach the end of the row, pass the needle around the last warp thread and bring it back up through the beads to secure them in place.

Weave Back: To begin the next row, weave the needle back through the beads in the opposite direction, passing over the beads you previously added and under the empty warp threads.

Continue Weaving: Repeat steps 3-9 for each subsequent row, alternating the direction of the weave with each pass to maintain the right-angle weave pattern.

Finishing Off: Once you've completed your desired length of beadwork, finish off the ends by weaving the thread through the beads to secure them in place. Secure the thread with a knot and trim any extra length.

CHAPTER FOUR

Beginner Projects

Beaded Bracelet

Materials Needed:

- Beading loom
- Beading thread or cord
- Beading needles
- Seed beads or other small beads
- Scissors
- Clasp or closure (optional)
- Beading mat or tray

Instructions:

Set up your loom according to the manufacturer's instructions and warp it with your desired thread or cord.

Choose your bead colors and thread them onto your beading needle in the desired pattern.

Begin weaving using the plain weave technique, following the instructions provided earlier.

Continue weaving until your bracelet reaches the desired length, keeping in mind the size of your wrist and any closures you plan to add.

Once you've completed the weaving, finish off the ends by weaving the thread through the beads to secure them in place. Secure the thread with a knot and trim any extra length.

If desired, add a clasp or closure to your bracelet for easy wear.

Your beaded bracelet is now complete and ready to wear or gift to someone special!

Beaded Bookmark

Materials Needed:

- Beading loom
- Beading thread or cord
- Beading needles
- Seed beads or other small beads
- Scissors
- Ribbon or tassel (optional)

Instructions:

Set up your loom and warp it with your chosen thread or cord, following the manufacturer's instructions.

Select your bead colors and thread them onto your beading needle in a pattern or design of your choice.

Begin weaving using the ladder stitch technique, as outlined earlier.

Weave until your bookmark reaches the desired length, keeping in mind the size of the book it will be used with.

Once you've finished weaving, secure the ends of the thread by weaving them back through the beads and tying them off.

If desired, add a decorative ribbon or tassel to one end of the bookmark for a finishing touch.

Your beaded bookmark is now ready to mark your place in your favorite book or to give as a thoughtful gift to a fellow book lover!

Beaded Earrings

Materials Needed:

- Beading loom
- Beading thread or cord
- Beading needles
- Seed beads or other small beads
- Earring hooks
- Jump rings (optional)
- Scissors
- Beading mat or tray

Instructions:

Set up your loom according to the manufacturer's instructions and warp it with your desired thread or cord.

Choose your bead colors and thread them onto your beading needle in the desired pattern.

Begin weaving using the ladder stitch or brick stitch technique, following the instructions provided earlier.

Weave until you've created a rectangular or square piece of beadwork that is slightly smaller than the size of your desired earring.

Once you've completed the weaving, finish off the ends by weaving the thread through the beads to secure them in place. Secure the thread with a knot and trim any extra length.

Attach an earring hook to the top of each beadwork piece using a jump ring if necessary.

Your beaded earrings are now complete and ready to wear or give as a stylish handmade gift!

Beaded Keychain

Materials Needed:

- Beading loom
- Beading thread or cord
- Beading needles
- Seed beads or other small beads
- Keychain ring
- Scissors
- Beading mat or tray

Instructions:

Set up your loom and warp it with your chosen thread or cord, following the manufacturer's instructions.

Select your bead colors and thread them onto your beading needle in a pattern or design of your choice.

Begin weaving using the ladder stitch or zigzag weave technique, as outlined earlier.

Weave until your beadwork piece is the desired length and width for your keychain.

Once you've finished weaving, secure the ends of the thread by weaving them back through the beads and tying them off.

Attach the beadwork piece to the keychain ring using a jump ring or by threading the ring through a loop of beads at one end of the beadwork.

Your beaded keychain is now ready to hold your keys in style or to give as a personalized gift to a friend or loved one!

Beaded Cell Phone Charm

Materials Needed:

- Beading loom
- Beading thread or cord
- Beading needles
- Seed beads or other small beads
- Jump rings
- Cell phone charm strap or lobster clasp
- Scissors
- Beading mat or tray

Instructions:

Set up your loom according to the manufacturer's instructions and warp it with your desired thread or cord.

Choose your bead colors and thread them onto your beading needle in the desired pattern.

Begin weaving using the ladder stitch or brick stitch technique, following the instructions provided earlier.

Weave until you've created a small rectangular or square piece of beadwork.

Once you've completed the weaving, finish off the ends by weaving the thread through the beads to secure them in place. Secure the thread with a knot and trim any extra length.

Attach a jump ring to one corner of the beadwork piece.

Attach the cell phone charm strap or lobster clasp to the jump ring.

Beaded Bookmark with Tassel

Materials Needed:

- Beading loom
- Beading thread or cord
- Beading needles
- Seed beads or other small beads
- Small piece of cardboard or cardstock
- Scissors
- Ribbon or embroidery floss
- Beading mat or tray

Instructions:

Set up your loom and warp it with your chosen thread or cord, following the manufacturer's instructions.

Select your bead colors and thread them onto your beading needle in a pattern or design of your choice.

Begin weaving using the ladder stitch or zigzag weave technique, as outlined earlier.

Weave until your bookmark is the desired length, leaving extra length at the ends for the tassel.

Once you've finished weaving, secure the ends of the thread by weaving them back through the beads and tying them off.

Cut a small piece of cardboard or cardstock to the desired length of your tassel. Wrap the embroidery floss or ribbon around the cardboard several times to create the tassel.

Slide the wrapped floss or ribbon off the cardboard and tie a knot at the top to secure it.

Attach the tassel to one end of the bookmark by threading the excess thread through the loop at the top of the tassel and tying it securely.

Cut the tassel ends to the preferred length.

Intermediate Projects

Beaded Cuff Bracelet

Materials Needed:

- Beading loom
- Beading thread or cord
- Beading needles
- Seed beads or other small beads
- Delica beads or larger accent beads
- Scissors
- Clasp or closure
- Beading mat or tray

Instructions:

Set up your loom according to the manufacturer's instructions and warp it with your desired thread or cord.

Choose your bead colors and thread them onto your beading needle in the desired pattern.

Begin weaving using a more intricate stitch such as the herringbone or peyote stitch, following the instructions provided earlier.

Experiment with adding different sizes and shapes of beads to create texture and dimension in your design.

Weave until your bracelet is the desired length, leaving extra length at each end for attaching the closure.

Once you've completed the weaving, finish off the ends by weaving the thread through the beads to secure them in place. Secure the thread with a knot and trim any extra length.

Attach a clasp or closure to each end of the bracelet using jump rings or by weaving the closure directly into the beadwork.

Beaded Pendant Necklace

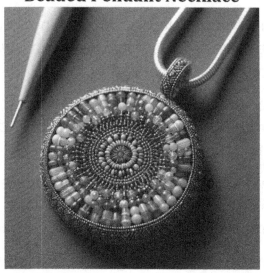

Materials Needed:

- Beading loom
- Beading thread or cord
- Beading needles
- Seed beads or other small beads
- Larger accent beads or focal bead
- Chain or cord for necklace
- Jump rings
- Clasp or closure
- Scissors
- Beading mat or tray

Instructions:

Set up your loom and warp it with your chosen thread or cord, following the manufacturer's instructions.

Select your bead colors and thread them onto your beading needle in a pattern or design of your choice.

Begin weaving using a more advanced stitch such as the St. Petersburg or right-angle weave, as outlined earlier.

Incorporate a larger accent bead or focal bead into your design to create a centerpiece for your pendant.

Weave until your pendant is the desired size and shape, keeping in mind the dimensions of your focal bead and the overall design of your necklace.

Once you've completed the weaving, finish off the ends by weaving the thread through the beads to secure them in place. Secure the thread with a knot and trim any extra length.

Attach a jump ring to the top of the pendant, and then attach the pendant to the chain or cord for your necklace using another jump ring.

Attach a clasp or closure to the ends of the chain or cord to complete the necklace.

Beaded Amulet Bag

Materials Needed:

- Beading loom
- Beading thread or cord
- Beading needles
- Seed beads or other small beads
- Larger accent beads or focal bead (optional)
- Scissors
- Beading mat or tray
- Beadwork pattern (optional)

Instructions:

Set up your loom according to the manufacturer's instructions and warp it with your desired thread or cord.

Choose your bead colors and thread them onto your beading needle in the desired pattern, or use a beadwork pattern for guidance.

Begin weaving using a more intricate stitch such as the peyote stitch, herringbone stitch, or right-angle weave, following the instructions provided earlier.

Experiment with adding larger accent beads or a focal bead to create a focal point for your amulet bag.

Weave until your amulet bag is the desired size and shape, leaving extra length at the top for closing the bag.

Once you've completed the weaving, finish off the ends by weaving the thread through the beads to secure them in place. Secure the thread with a knot and trim any extra length.

Fold the beadwork in half to create the front and back of the bag, and stitch the sides together using a ladder stitch or whip stitch.

Attach a small loop or ring to the top of the bag for attaching a cord or chain.

Beaded Picture Frame

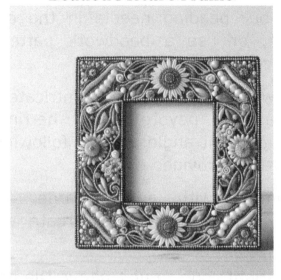

Materials Needed:

- Beading loom
- Beading thread or cord
- Beading needles
- Seed beads or other small beads
- Small picture frame
- Craft glue
- Scissors
- Beading mat or tray

Instructions:

Set up your loom and warp it with your chosen thread or cord, following the manufacturer's instructions.

Select your bead colors and thread them onto your beading needle in a pattern or design of your choice.

Begin weaving using a variety of bead weaving stitches such as the peyote stitch, herringbone stitch, or brick stitch, as outlined earlier.

Weave a piece of beadwork that is slightly larger than the opening of your picture frame.

Once you've completed the weaving, finish off the ends by weaving the thread through the beads to secure them in place. Secure the thread with a knot and trim any extra length.

Apply a thin layer of craft glue to the front of the picture frame, covering the entire surface.

Carefully place the beadwork onto the glued surface of the picture frame, pressing down gently to adhere it in place.

Let the glue dry fully as per the instructions provided by the manufacturer.

Once the glue is dry, trim any excess beadwork from around the edges of the picture frame using scissors.

Advanced Projects

Beaded Tapestry Wall Hanging

Materials Needed:

- Beading loom
- Beading thread or cord
- Beading needles
- Seed beads or other small beads in various colors
- Larger accent beads or focal beads
- Wooden dowel or rod
- Scissors
- Craft glue
- Beading mat or tray

Instructions:

Set up your loom according to the manufacturer's instructions and warp it with your desired thread or cord.

Choose a design for your tapestry wall hanging and create a pattern on graph paper or using a computer design program.

Begin weaving your design using various bead weaving techniques such as the peyote stitch, loom weaving, or brick stitch, following your pattern.

Experiment with adding larger accent beads or focal beads to create texture and dimension in your tapestry.

Weave until your tapestry is the desired size and shape, leaving extra length at the top for attaching to the wooden dowel.

Once you've completed the weaving, finish off the ends by weaving the thread through the beads to secure them in place. Secure the thread with a knot and trim any extra length.

Apply a thin layer of craft glue to the top edge of the tapestry and press it onto the wooden dowel, allowing the glue to dry completely.

Attach a piece of string or cord to each end of the wooden dowel for hanging your tapestry on the wall.

Beaded Statement Necklace with Matching Earrings

Materials Needed:

- Beading loom
- Beading thread or cord
- Beading needles
- Seed beads or other small beads in various colors
- Larger accent beads or focal beads
- Jewelry findings (necklace clasp, earring hooks, jump rings)

- Scissors
- Jewelry pliers
- Beading mat or tray

Instructions:

Set up your loom and warp it with your chosen thread or cord, following the manufacturer's instructions.

Select a design for your statement necklace and create a pattern on graph paper or using a computer design program.

Begin weaving your necklace using various bead weaving techniques such as the St. Petersburg stitch, right-angle weave, or herringbone stitch, following your pattern.

Experiment with adding larger accent beads or focal beads to create a focal point for your necklace.

Weave until your necklace is the desired length, leaving extra length at each end for attaching the clasp.

Once you've completed the weaving, finish off the ends by weaving the thread through the beads to secure them in place. Secure the thread with a knot and trim any extra length.

Attach a necklace clasp to each end of the necklace using jump rings and jewelry pliers.

To create matching earrings, repeat the weaving process using a smaller version of the necklace design.

Attach earring hooks to each earring using jump rings and jewelry pliers.

Beaded Amulet Necklace with Fringe

Materials Needed:

- Beading loom
- Beading thread or cord
- Beading needles

- Seed beads or other small beads in various colors
- Larger accent beads or focal beads
- Small charms or pendants
- Chain or cord for necklace
- Jump rings
- Clasp or closure
- Scissors
- Beading mat or tray

Instructions:

Set up your loom according to the manufacturer's instructions and warp it with your desired thread or cord.

Choose a design for your amulet necklace and create a pattern on graph paper or using a computer design program.

Begin weaving your design using various bead weaving techniques such as the peyote stitch, loom weaving, or brick stitch, following your pattern.

Experiment with adding larger accent beads or focal beads to create a focal point for your necklace.

Weave until your amulet is the desired size and shape, leaving extra length at the top for attaching to the necklace chain.

Once you've completed the weaving, finish off the ends by weaving the thread through the beads to secure them in place. Secure the thread with a knot and trim any extra length.

Attach small charms or pendants to the bottom edge of the amulet using jump rings.

Attach the amulet to the necklace chain using jump rings, ensuring it is centered.

Attach a clasp or closure to the ends of the necklace chain to complete the necklace.

Optional: Add fringe to the bottom edge of the amulet by threading beads onto short lengths of thread and attaching them to the bottom row of beads.

Beaded Statement Cuff Bracelet

Materials Needed:

- Beading loom
- Beading thread or cord
- Beading needles
- Seed beads or other small beads in various colors
- Larger accent beads or focal beads
- Ribbon or fabric for backing
- Glue
- Scissors
- Beading mat or tray

Instructions:

Set up your loom according to the manufacturer's instructions and warp it with your desired thread or cord.

Choose a design for your cuff bracelet and create a pattern on graph paper or using a computer design program.

Begin weaving your design using various bead weaving techniques such as the peyote stitch, loom weaving, or brick stitch, following your pattern.

Experiment with adding larger accent beads or focal beads to create a focal point for your bracelet.

Weave until your bracelet is the desired size and shape, ensuring it will fit comfortably around your wrist.

Once you've completed the weaving, remove it from the loom and trim any excess thread.

Glue the beadwork onto a piece of ribbon or fabric for backing, ensuring it is centered and secure.

Allow the glue to dry completely before wearing your bracelet.

Optional: Add additional embellishments such as fringe, tassels, or charms to customize your bracelet further.

Beaded Mandala Wall Art

Materials Needed:

- Beading loom
- Beading thread or cord
- Beading needles
- Seed beads or other small beads in various colors
- Larger accent beads or focal beads
- Wooden hoop or embroidery hoop
- Fabric backing
- Craft glue

- Scissors
- Beading mat or tray

Instructions:

Set up your loom according to the manufacturer's instructions and warp it with your desired thread or cord.

Choose a mandala design or create your own pattern on graph paper or using a computer design program.

Begin weaving your mandala design using various bead weaving techniques such as the peyote stitch, loom weaving, or brick stitch, following your pattern.

Experiment with adding larger accent beads or focal beads to create texture and dimension in your mandala.

Weave until your mandala is the desired size and shape, ensuring it will fit within the wooden hoop or embroidery hoop.

Once you've completed the weaving, remove it from the loom and trim any excess thread.

Glue the beadwork onto a fabric backing, ensuring it is centered and secure.

Place the fabric backing with the beadwork into the wooden hoop or embroidery hoop, pulling the fabric taut and tightening the hoop to secure it in place.

Allow the glue to dry completely before displaying your beaded mandala wall art.

Beaded Bridal Headpiece

Materials Needed:

- Beading loom
- Beading thread or cord
- Beading needles
- Seed beads or other small beads in ivory or white
- Larger accent beads or crystals

- Metal headband or hair comb
- Ribbon or fabric for backing
- Craft glue
- Scissors
- Beading mat or tray

Instructions:

Set up your loom according to the manufacturer's instructions and warp it with your desired thread or cord.

Choose a design for your bridal headpiece, such as a floral motif or geometric pattern, and create a pattern on graph paper or using a computer design program.

Begin weaving your headpiece design using various bead weaving techniques such as the peyote stitch, loom weaving, or brick stitch, following your pattern.

Use ivory or white beads for the main body of the headpiece and add larger accent beads or crystals for extra sparkle and dimension.

Weave until your headpiece is the desired size and shape, ensuring it will fit comfortably on the headband or hair comb.

Once you've completed the weaving, remove it from the loom and trim any excess thread.

Glue the beadwork onto a piece of ribbon or fabric for backing, ensuring it is centered and secure.

Attach the beadwork to the metal headband or hair comb using craft glue, making sure it is positioned securely.

Allow the glue to dry completely before wearing your beaded bridal headpiece on your special day.

CHAPTER FIVE

Troubleshooting

Uneven tension: If your beadwork appears uneven or distorted, it may be due to uneven tension in the warp threads. Make sure the tension on all the warp threads is consistent by adjusting the tension knobs on your loom if necessary.

Beads not sitting properly: If your beads are not sitting properly or are unevenly spaced, it may be due to using beads of inconsistent size or shape. Sort through your beads and remove any that are significantly different in size or shape to ensure a uniform appearance.

Thread breakage: If your beading thread keeps breaking, it may be due to using thread that is too thin or weak for the weight of your beads. Consider using a stronger, thicker thread or doubling up on your thread for added strength.

Difficulty threading the needle: If you're having trouble threading your beading needle, try using a needle with a larger eye or flattening the end of the thread with a pair of pliers to make it easier to thread.

Beads falling off the loom: If your beads keep slipping off the loom while you're weaving, it may be due to not securing the end of the thread properly. Make sure to tie a secure knot at the end of your thread before beginning to weave, and periodically check to make sure the knots are still secure as you work.

Difficulty maintaining the pattern: If you're having trouble maintaining the pattern of your beadwork, try using a beadwork pattern or chart to help guide your weaving. You can also use markers or highlighters to mark your place in the pattern as you work.

Finishing off the ends: If you're unsure how to finish off the ends of your beadwork, consider using a beading needle to weave the thread back through the beads several times to secure them in place. You can also tie off the thread with a secure knot and trim any excess.

By troubleshooting these common issues, you can improve your bead weaving skills and create beautiful beadwork with ease!

General Tips

Start with a simple project: If you're new to bead weaving, start with a simple project to familiarize yourself with the process and techniques before attempting more complex designs.

Use quality materials: Choose high-quality beads, thread, and other materials for your bead weaving projects to ensure durability and a professional finish.

Follow the instructions: Read and follow the manufacturer's instructions for setting up and using your bead loom to ensure proper operation and best results.

Practice good tension: Maintain even tension on your warp threads and weaving thread to create uniform and professional-looking beadwork.

Experiment with different stitches: Explore different bead weaving stitches such as peyote stitch, brick stitch, and right-angle weave to create a variety of textures and patterns in your beadwork.

Keep your work area organized: Use a beading mat or tray to keep your beads and tools organized and prevent them from rolling away or getting lost.

Take breaks: Bead weaving can be time-consuming and repetitive, so take regular breaks to rest your eyes and hands and prevent fatigue.

Pay attention to detail: Pay attention to detail and take your time to ensure each bead is positioned correctly and each stitch is made accurately for a polished finished product.

Experiment with color and texture: Have fun experimenting with different bead colors, finishes, and textures to create unique and personalized beadwork.

Don't be afraid to make mistakes: Mistakes are a natural part of the learning process, so don't be afraid to make them! Use mistakes as opportunities to learn and improve your bead weaving skills.

By following these general tips, you can enhance your bead weaving experience and create beautiful beadwork with confidence and creativity!

CONCLUSION

Bead weaving on a loom is a versatile and rewarding craft that offers endless opportunities for creativity and self-expression. Whether you're a beginner just starting out or an experienced crafter looking to expand your skills, bead weaving provides a satisfying outlet for artistic exploration.

Throughout this book, we've covered everything you need to know to get started with bead weaving on a loom, from the history and benefits of the craft to essential materials and tools, setting up your workspace, and mastering basic and advanced techniques. We've also provided step-by-step instructions for a variety of beginner, intermediate, and advanced projects, allowing you to put your newfound skills into practice and create beautiful handmade jewelry, accessories, and decor.

Thank you for joining us on this bead weaving adventure. We hope you've found this book informative and inspiring, and we can't wait to see the beautiful beadwork you create!

Made in the USA
Monee, IL
11 November 2024

69871439R00046